★ ★

INDIANS OF AMERICA

Crazy Horse

WAR CHIEF OF THE OGLALA

MATTHEW G. GRANT

Illustrated by John Keely and Dick Brude

GALLERY OF GREAT AMERICANS SERIES

★ ★

Crazy Horse

WAR CHIEF OF THE OGLALA

Library of Congress Number: 73-12403

ISBN: O-87191-269-4

Published by Creative Education, Mankato, Minnesota 56001
Distributed by Childrens Press, 1224 West Van Buren Street,
Chicago, Illinois 60607

Library of Congress Cataloging in Publication Data
  Grant, Matthew G
    Crazy Horse, war chief of the Oglala.
    (His Indians of America) (Gallery of great Americans series)
    SUMMARY: A brief biography of the Oglala Sioux leader whose resistance to the army's attempt to move his people to a reservation resulted in Custer's defeat at Little Bighorn and his own premature death.
    1. Crazy Horse, Oglala Indian, 1842(ca.)-1877—Juvenile literature. [1. Crazy Horse, Oglala Indian, 1842(ca)-1877. 2. Dakota Indians—Biography. 3. Indians of North America—Biography] I. Keely, John, illus. II. Brode, Dick, illus. III. Title.
E99.03C723 970.3 [B] [92] 73-12403 ISBN 0-87191-269-4

CONTENTS

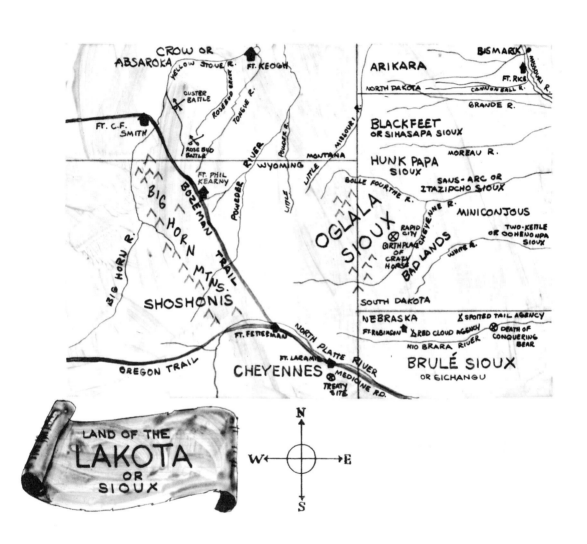

CROW OR
ABSAROKA
YELLOW STONE R.   FT. KEOGH
CUSTER
BATTLE
ROSEBUD CREEK
TONGUE R.
FT. C.F.
SMITH
ROSE BUD
BATTLE
POWDER R.
BOZEMAN TRAIL
FT. PHIL
KEARNY
POWDER RIVER
WYOMING
MONTANA
LITTLE
LITTLE
BIG
HORN
MTNS.
BIG HORN R.
SHOSHONIS
FT. FETTERMAN
NORTH PLATTE RIVER
OREGON TRAIL
CHEYENNES
MEDICINE RD.
FT. LARAMIE
TREATY
SITE

BISMARK
MISSOURI R.
ARIKARA
FT. RICE
NORTH DAKOTA
CANNON BALL R.
GRANDE R.
BLACKFEET
OR SIHASAPA SIOUX
MOREAU R.
MISSOURI R.
HUNK PAPA
SIOUX
SANS-ARC OR
ITAZIPCHO SIOUX
BELLE FOURTHE R.
MINICONJOUS
OGLALA
SIOUX
RAPID
CITY
BIRTHPLACE
OF
CRAZY
HORSE
CHEYENNE R.
TWO-KETTLE
OR OOHENONPA
SIOUX
BAD LANDS
WHITE R.
SOUTH DAKOTA
NEBRASKA
SPOTTED TAIL AGENCY
FT. ROBINSON
RED CLOUD AGENCY
DEATH OF
CONQUERING
BEAR
NIO BRARA RIVER
BRULÉ SIOUX
OR SICHANGU

LAND OF THE
LAKOTA
OR
SIOUX

N
W ← → E
S

TROUBLE ON MEDICINE ROAD

Of all the Plains Indians, the most fierce and most numerous were the Lakota. White men called them the Sioux. There were seven tribes in the Sioux nation. One of the largest was the Oglala.

The Oglala were great horseback riders and warriors. They planted no crops and built no towns. Herds of buffalo gave them food, clothing, and most of the other things they needed to live.

About 1841, a son was born to Crazy Horse, a holy man or shaman of the Oglala. The boy had fine brown hair and they called him Curly. When he was still very small, Curly decided to become a warrior.

A warrior named Hump became Curly's "older brother," teaching him to hunt and fight. When Curly was ten, Hump took him to the great council at Fort Laramie. There the white soldiers said that the Indians would be given presents if they kept the peace. The Indians were not to molest white travelers on the Medicine Road — the Oregon Trail. Some Indians signed the treaty. Most did not understand it.

In 1854, when Curly was about 13, there was trouble along the Medicine Road. A white settler said that an Indian stole his cow. Chief Conquering Bear tried to tell a white army officer that it was all a mistake.

The officer misunderstood. He told his troops to fire on the Indians. The chief fell dead and the angry Indians killed all the soldiers.

Young Curly began to feel hate for white men.

When Curly was 14, he went on his Vision Quest. He asked God to give him a dream of power. The boy dreamed of a storm and a hawk. His father said this meant he would lead his people in battle.

Hump took Curly on his first raid a few years later. The boy fought bravely against the Grass House Indians. The tribe proclaimed him a man. And Curly received his father's name, Crazy Horse.

SIOUX ON THE WARPATH

Years passed. Crazy Horse became a great warrior. His battles were mostly with other Indian tribes. But he often heard about Indians and whites fighting to the south.

15

One day, messenger brought bad news. White soldiers had attacked a peaceful village, killing 100 families. Hump, Crazy Horse, and many other Oglalas joined a group of Sioux that declared war on the whites.

The Sioux Wars began about 1865. For three years the Indians fought the U.S. Army. Crazy Horse became a war leader of one large group. Chief Sitting Bull led another.

The U.S. Government tried to make peace by giving the Indians a huge reservation in 1868. "All this land shall be yours," the white men said, "as long as the grass shall grow and the water flow.''

Some Indians believed it. But not Crazy Horse and Sitting Bull. Their people kept on fighting. They had only scorn for the reservation Indians. How could white men give them land that was already theirs?

THE LITTLE BIG HORN

By 1875, Crazy Horse was chief of a large band of Oglalas. They heard that the U.S. Government was trying to force the Sioux to sell part of their big reservation — the holy Black Hills country.

General Crook retreated and called for more men. The Indians moved their camp to the Little Big Horn River and waited.

A week later, an army officer named George Armstrong Custer disobeyed orders and attacked the Indian camp with a force of less than 700 men.

Crazy Horse led 3,000 Indians to the attack. He cried: "Come on! This is a good day to die!"

This was the land that was to belong to the red men "as long as the grass shall grow." So much for white promises!

Crazy Horse and his people joined Sitting Bull and other Indian leaders for a last stand against the white army. About 1,000 Indians, led by Crazy Horse and Sitting Bull, fought General Crook's men at Rosebud Creek, June 17, 1876. The Indians won.

The ones who died were Custer and more than 200 of his men. Crazy Horse killed many but he himself was not wounded. He was protected by the magic hailstones painted on his body in honor of his Storm Vision.

After the victory, Crazy Horse and the other leaders met with Sitting Bull, who was leader of all the Sioux. Another white army was coming. It was time for the Indians to disappear.

Sitting Bull wanted the Indians to go to Canada. But it was a long way. Many of the people did not want to leave the country they had fought so hard for.

Crazy Horse led one large group and Sitting Bull another. They bade each other farewell. Sitting Bull went north while Crazy Horse went south and then east, back to the Black Hills. He and his young men took up their war against the settlers again.

A large white army under General Nelson A. Miles pursued the Indians. Many were captured and sent to the reservation. But Crazy Horse and his people still fought through the summer and fall.

Then came the winter, one of the worst the Indians had known. Buffalo were scarce and the people were very hungry. In January 1877 General Miles attacked Crazy Horse's camp. The people fled.

CONQUEST OF THE SIOUX

The Indians had no more bullets or gun-powder. Their great victory on the Little Big Horn had been a black one, a last bit of glory before the end. Even brave Crazy Horse knew what would soon happen.

Starving and freezing, the Oglalas were chased over the frozen plains. Often the white men sent them messages: "Come into the reservation."

The people were losing heart. And Crazy Horse's own wife, Black Shawl, was sick with the coughing disease.

Old Indian friends came to Crazy Horse and begged him to give up. At last the chief agreed. It was the only way he could save his people from death.

On May 6, 1877, Crazy Horse surrendered at Fort Robinson, Nebraska. He brought about 1,000 of his people into the Red Cloud Agency. The white leaders promised Crazy Horse an agency of his own. They said he would be allowed to go to Washington and talk to the Great Father about his people.

But this promise was not kept. Some of the Sioux on the reservation made trouble for Crazy Horse.

Indians who were jealous told the whites that Crazy Horse was going to lead a revolt. September 4, when the chief brought his sick wife to visit her family, he was arrested.

Red men who hated him grabbed his arms. White soldiers who thought he was escaping stabbed him. He died the next day. His sorrowing people hid his body where whites would never find it.

★ ★

GALLERY OF GREAT AMERICANS SERIES

★ ★

INDIANS OF AMERICA
GERONIMO
CRAZY HORSE
CHIEF JOSEPH
PONTIAC
SQUANTO
OSCEOLA

EXPLORERS OF AMERICA
COLUMBUS
LEIF ERICKSEN
DeSOTO
LEWIS AND CLARK
CHAMPLAIN
CORONADO

FRONTIERSMEN OF AMERICA
DANIEL BOONE
BUFFALO BILL
JIM BRIDGER
FRANCIS MARION
DAVY CROCKET
KIT CARSON

WAR HEROES OF AMERICA
JOHN PAUL JONES
PAUL REVERE
ROBERT E. LEE
ULYSSES S. GRANT
SAM HOUSTON
LAFAYETTE

WOMEN OF AMERICA
CLARA BARTON
JANE ADAMS
ELIZABETH BLACKWELL
HARRIET TUBMAN
SUSAN B. ANTHONY
DOLLY MADISON

★ ★